FRANZ FERDINAND

NICHOLAS ARTSRUNIK

artnik books

FRANZ
FERDINAND

First published in Great Britain in 2005
by Artnik
341b Queenstown Road
London SW8 4LH
UK

ISBN 1-905382-00-6

Design: Supriya Sahai
Pictures: Live Photography
Editor: John McVicar
Researcher: Kirsty Morgan

Printed and bound in Spain
by Gráficas Díaz

To **Nicholas Kaye**, who always laid claim to the dedication of my first book.
For being the first to think that I had any sort of talent.

Aknowledgements
John McVicar
Charles Conway

These publications were invaluable to my research:
www.franzferdinand.org
www.geocities.com/franzferdinand
www.xs4all.nl

I would also like to credit the following assortment of riff-raff, even though they (really) don't deserve it:

Rosie – Voila 'le livre truque'
Sibley – I am now the walking encyclopaedia
Libs – Whose conversation helped me with everything apart from this book
'One Can' Sam – See you in bonny Scotland
Poppy Dave – F**k Forever
Alex - Sexy Mormons

Logger – Blazin' on a sunny afternoon
Heed Mathewson – Keep trying, mate…just generally
JonanAmy – Get off our damn sofas
Doive
Lorcan 'the Dinosaur'

The Magic Tree Crew
Girl By The Tree – uh…Claire??
Big Pete – Big hands…big feet
Mayhew – I heard your songs on MTV…

The Amateur Transplants – Who amused me when nothing else was funny

All the people and institutions that I secretly laugh at.

'I am the new Scottish gentry,' announces Alex Kapranos during 'Shopping for Blood', which is a blitzkrieg on the anglofication of Scotland. He sings in a perfect pitch that complements his sartorial sharpness on a night when his band, Franz Ferdinand, will begin to make its name in the history of rock 'n' roll as indelible as the assassination of their namesake did in the history of war.

As Nick begins his ascent into the instrumental chaos that is the climax to 'Darts of Pleasure', Alex examines his audience. He is steeled against disappointment – after all this is Oxford, not the Château, which would by now would be packed with all the trendsetting art students of Glasgow. Scanning the room, he clocks Annie Lennox, the ex-lead singer of the Eurythmics and still a rock 'n' roll icon.

SHE IS DANCING AND SINGING ALONG TO NICK'S BIZARRE CHORUS– 'ICH HEISSE SUPER FANTASTIK'. HIS HEAD ROCKS BACK IN AMAZEMENT.

At the end of the number, he dedicates the set to everyone who is dancing, then as he sees the excited eyes and hears the rapturous cheers he feels the G-force of lift-off. Franz, he knows, is on its way; the band is taking off. Next stop, the Capithole itself. **Art-rock had been born.**

Alex Kapranos, the dapper, self-professed 'gentleman of the band', was born Alexander Paul Kapranos Huntley on the 20 March 1972. If an interviewer asks the date of his birth, he always replies, 'Sometime in the late twentieth century.' Rock 'n' roll is the preserve of the young. Its stars have usually staked out their position in the firmament by their mid-twenties. Alex was going to make it but he wasn't sure if it was cool to have waited so long.

Born in Almondsbury, Gloucestershire, he was the son of a British mother and a Greek father who had been adopted by a British family named 'Huntley'. Alex actually lived in Greece until he was two years old, when his mother decided she could no longer stand the blast-furnace heat. The family duly switched to the other extreme, moving to the cold, damp north-east of England where Alex's grandmother lived. The switch in climate made him asthmatic and, even today, he is never without an inhaler.

His father John Huntley became a successful legal academic and is now a professor at Caledonian University, Glasgow. When they returned from Greece, the family settled in Washington on Tyneside. The boy got his first dose of education at the Redby Primary School in Sunderland.

Childhood can be tough on a young kid growing up in the North East with a foreign background and who finds he is useless at football. Alex was never a physical boy and even his grandmother remembers him as 'a weedy child who disliked sports'. To compensate for this, however, Alex developed a strong interest in music. His grandmother recalls, 'He was always into his music and always fancied playing the guitar and he had piano lessons when he was a child. **His dad was always quite musical as well**.'

His parents moved to live in Sunderland briefly when he was 12 years old but, at 14, the family moved north of the border to Glasgow, which quickly became Alex's adopted home town. He is now quick to admit that the mid-80s, early 90s music scene in Glasgow gave him a lot of inspiration to write his own songs. Freed from what Alex would call the oppressive influence of the **'Capithole'** (London), Glaswegian rock bands special-ised in a unique form of feel-good punk music that would have you tapping your feet and make you think. Yet, Alex always decries the idea that rock lyrics should make you think and even now argues that **'pop music is music that moves you without engaging the brain, and then allows you to engage the brain afterwards**.' But he says a lot things that he doesn't really mean.

Unfortunately his obsession with musicianship and song writing clashed with meeting the demands of his education and even in relation to what he was already specialising in, music, he was hardly being hailed as the new Mozart. His music teacher bluntly told his parents that he was 'musically inept'. Whilst this didn't stop Alex's interest in the subject or, indeed, the practice of writing music, it did lead to a change in how he viewed his future.

'WHEN YOU'RE LITTLE, YOU DREAM OF GOING ON *TOP OF THE POPS*, BUT ONLY IN THE SAME WAY YOU DREAM OF BEING A TRAIN DRIVER OR AN ASTRONAUT,' Kapranos admits. 'BUT PLAYING MUSIC DID SEEM LIKE A BIT OF A LAUGH.'

Alex began his time at university as a student of Divinity/Theology at Aberdeen. Exactly why he decided to embark upon this course is a mystery that he has never cleared up. He probably fancied himself as sleeper for Satan who would plant himself in the Church before rising up within to destroy it. Either he became disillusioned with his mission or bored with the lessons for within 6 months he had switched both course and location to study English Literature at Glasgow.

As a career move, this was possibly not the best decision to make for a middle-class Glaswegian who still entertained dreams of emulating late 70s' underground rock bands such as the Fire Engines, although Alex did end up becoming a rock star rather than some missionary for Satan. When he left university, however, he found that an English Lit degree didn't have much clout in the job market. Desperate to earn some money, he began the long march to his pension by **becoming a dish washer**. **Then as a welder. Next as a delivery boy...**

In fact, he worked in almost any detestable job he could find, although the delivery boy job for Mother India's café was an exception. As part of his pay he got a free meal, which left him with a chilli habit that Alex still indulges enthusiastically:

'I would probably have done it for the food alone. I go through periods of compulsive addiction to chillies. I think you build up immunity to the heat.

Like the ancient Peruvians he reveres the chilli as a sacred gift from the gods. He believes that earning a pound for each takeaway that he delivered was his rite de passage to becoming a millionaire rock star. '**I delivered the food of the gods to a race that was dying the death of a thousand fried Mars bars a day.**'

By far his most interesting job outside of the music scene was a humanitarian one after the war in Kosovo. Alex drove a Land Rover ambulance the 1,500 miles to the ex-Yugoslavian province.

The big problem with all these dead end jobs was not so much the poor pay as how it curtailed his involvement in Glasgow's thriving underground music scene. As a student, this had been his raison d'etre. However, he picked up the real threads of his life again when he began working as a promoter for the downmarket 13th Note Club. Alex ran two club nights a week: the Kazoo Club and the 99P Club. The latter was named such because, unlike the former, which was free, the young entrepreneur would charge a pound per person as an entrance fee.

'The idea was the bands would come down and play for a bit of beer,' he recalls, 'and people wouldn't have to pay and we'd give 'em amps to play with and stuff. And the 99P Club, we just charged a quid to get in and the band got the money. It was just a good sort of environment. Lots of people got together. **It was a good scene.**'

'I'M AT THE STAGE WHERE I NEED TO STICK THREE CHILLIES ON A SLICE OF CHEESE ON TOAST BEFORE I CAN TASTE THEM.'

Alex, who was by now a talented musician, having taught himself to play bass and guitar, joined in with many of the bands he booked at the 13th Note. He played alongside groups such as the 10P Invaders, the Amphetameanies, and sang a song for The Catterson Quartet. Alex actually appeared on Glasgow group Quinn's first album, *In Between Worlds*, as a guitarist.

He formed his first band in 1996 as the lead singer, going under the name of Alex Huntley. The band was called the **Blisters**, although they were later renamed **The Karelia**, and released their only album, *Divorce at High Noon* in 1997.

The sharp-suited quartet were heavily influenced by cult 80s band The Monochrome Set, 1920s jazz and pre-war French balladeers and, as such, didn't exactly set the charts alight. Nevertheless, some connection to the Franz Ferdinand sound to come can be detected, not least in Alex's lyrics which already flirt with the arch wordplay he would later finesse into what is the hallmark of FF.

The other members of the group were Glen Thomson (now the tour manager of Franz Ferdinand), Allan Wylie and the exotically named Tassos Bombos. Needless to say, the project collapsed as record label Roadrunner dropped Alex and his group, when the album caused barely a ripple in the music industry. To avenge this unceremonious parting of ways, Alex jumped on the band wagon of the Yummy Fur, named after a Canadian comic strip, in 1998.

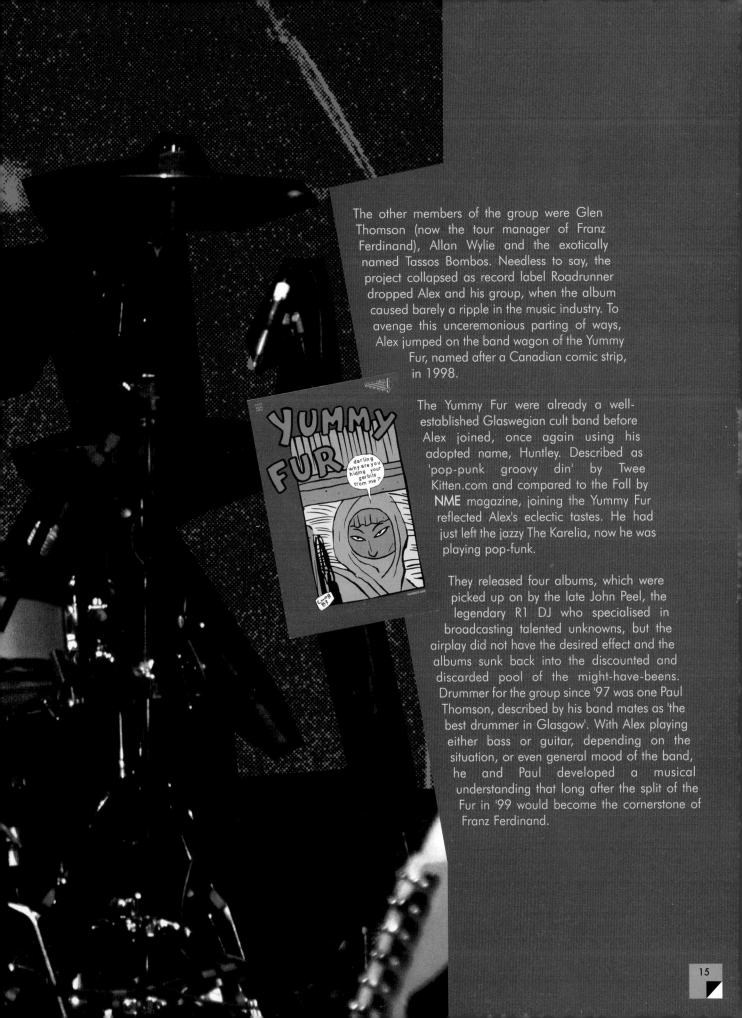

The Yummy Fur were already a well-established Glaswegian cult band before Alex joined, once again using his adopted name, Huntley. Described as 'pop-punk groovy din' by Twee Kitten.com and compared to the Fall by **NME** magazine, joining the Yummy Fur reflected Alex's eclectic tastes. He had just left the jazzy The Karelia, now he was playing pop-funk.

They released four albums, which were picked up on by the late John Peel, the legendary R1 DJ who specialised in broadcasting talented unknowns, but the airplay did not have the desired effect and the albums sunk back into the discounted and discarded pool of the might-have-beens. Drummer for the group since '97 was one Paul Thomson, described by his band mates as 'the best drummer in Glasgow'. With Alex playing either bass or guitar, depending on the situation, or even general mood of the band, he and Paul developed a musical understanding that long after the split of the Fur in '99 would become the cornerstone of Franz Ferdinand.

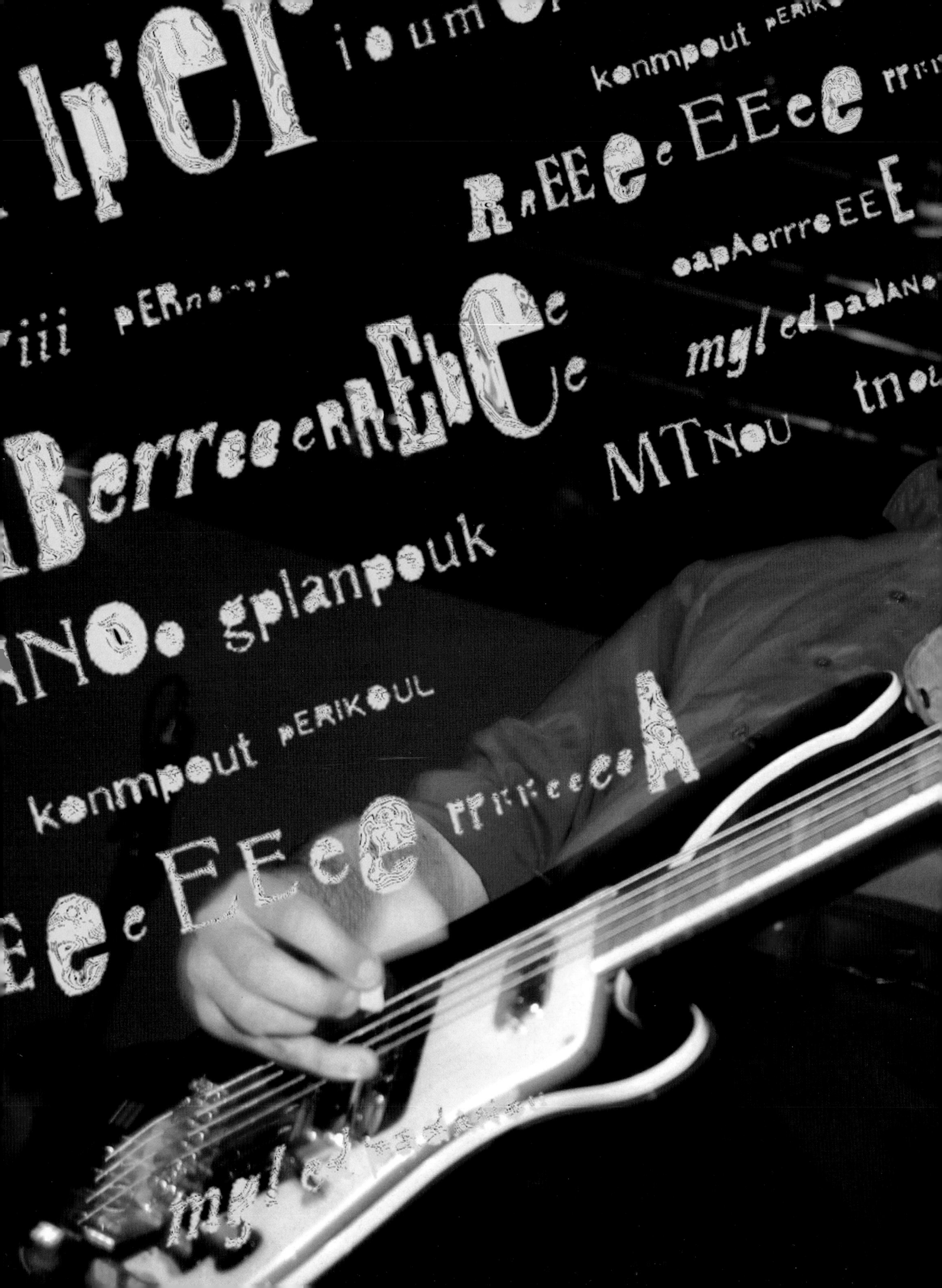

Paul Robert Thomson was born in Duddingston, Edinburgh on 15 September 1976, making him officially the youngest and only Scottish member of the band. As a child he choked on a button and retains an irrational fear for flat, round objects, except if they are coins. He studied Environmental Art at the Glasgow School of Art, obtaining a Ph.D., yet had always been interested in music. With the Yummy Fur he had experimented with various instruments, including guitars, bass guitars, drums, and keyboards.

Paul's first gig with the Fur had ended in drunken embarrassment. He had calmed his pre-gig nerves by swigging the 'rider' – free booze laid on for the band by the gig's promoter:

'We had the biggest rider ever – vodka, whisky, gin, cava, white wine, red wine and beer. I decided to sample some of each before going on."

Paul staggered on stage at the start of the gig, mumbled a few words and promptly plunged headfirst into the crowd as his proud mum, sister and cousins stood cringing in the crowd.

'I GOT THROWN OUT THREE TIMES, EACH TIME I WOULD JUST LET MYSELF IN THROUGH THE BACK DOOR.'

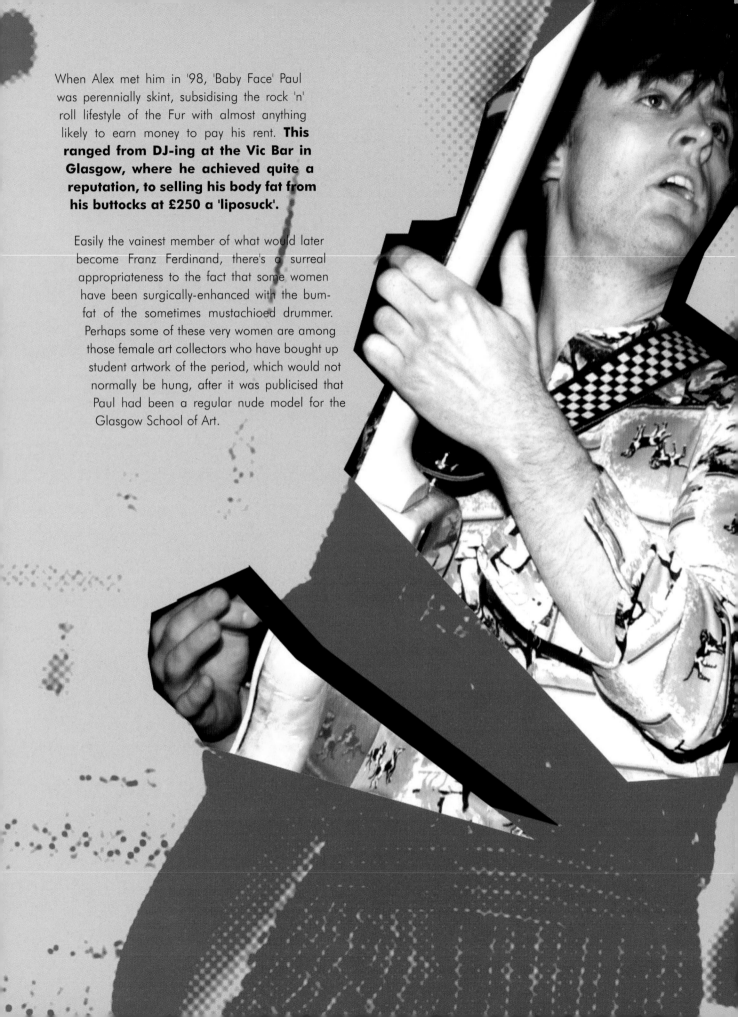

When Alex met him in '98, 'Baby Face' Paul was perennially skint, subsidising the rock 'n' roll lifestyle of the Fur with almost anything likely to earn money to pay his rent. **This ranged from DJ-ing at the Vic Bar in Glasgow, where he achieved quite a reputation, to selling his body fat from his buttocks at £250 a 'liposuck'.**

Easily the vainest member of what would later become Franz Ferdinand, there's a surreal appropriateness to the fact that some women have been surgically-enhanced with the bum-fat of the sometimes mustachioed drummer. Perhaps some of these very women are among those female art collectors who have bought up student artwork of the period, which would not normally be hung, after it was publicised that Paul had been a regular nude model for the Glasgow School of Art.

It was Alex who duly revealed this fact to the press: 'There will be all of these third and fourth year students and above at the art school with nude pictures of Paul. He told us about one where he was asked to sit in a Christine Keeler pose, but the chair was backless. You can imagine the crudeness of the drawings which exist of Paul in that pose.

I'M SURE THEY'LL SURFACE AT SOME POINT. ALL OF OUR GIRL FRIENDS HAD DRAWN PAUL IN THE NUDE.

'That is the thing that bonded us together as a band. Can you imagine what it does for your libido to go into your girlfriend's bedroom and see a nude portrait of Paul on the wall? Though Paul doesn't seem to mind, he is quite proud of his assets.'

When the Yummy Fur split in 1999 without releasing a single record on which Alex appeared, Paul turned to his own project, Pro Forma, with whom he continued to play until 2002. Alex, however, was now 27, and didn't want to be approaching his thirties as a down-and-out musician with no hope of a future except as a session man.

On an impulse, to develop an option on an alternative career, he took a job as a commis chef in a contemporary, club-cum-restaurant called Grouch Saint Jude's. After a short time working in the kitchens, he helped an art student friend of his, Bob Hardy, get a similar job in the restaurant:

'I worked with Bob; we were both Chefs. The head chef was a very cool Australian called Martin Teplitzsky who ran a very rock 'n' roll kitchen, knives and brandy would fly as the Stooges and Velvet Underground played during servings.'

In late 2001, the first seed of what would become Franz Ferdinand was sown.

Alex had just finished yet another week of meaningless work at the Grouch Saint Jude's and had become disillusioned with the prospect of working in kitchens for the rest of his life. The more he was away from it, the more he missed it. Music had to be a big part of his life. He had begun to search for other jobs that would give him more time to pursue his musical interests. So far, he had found one strong possibility: a vacancy at Anniesland College to teach English and Information Technology to asylum seekers. On the day he went for a job interview, he decided to return to the 13th Note Club again, which he did from time to time. He liked to keep up with the new array of talent in Glasgow, as well as see the struggling musicians whose company he used to keep and, to some extent, still did.

Alex was pleased to see Mick Cooke of seven piece folk-rock band Belle & Sebastian at the Club. The trumpeter was now playing for various other bands, including one Alex himself once played for, a ska group called the Amphetameanies.

Belle & Sebastian was a firm fixture on Alex's list of favourite bands. Playing a mixture of 60s pop and folk rock, these 'Scottish troubadours' as they were called would later become one of the few bands that Franz Ferdinand would name as inspirations for their own sound.

'Bands like Belle & Sebastian show you that you can retain your independence, do things your own way and succeed.'

This night, however, Mick gave Alex a bass guitar on the condition that he 'did something useful' with it. The gesture touched Alex and he resolved to try again to form a successful band.

Later in the evening, when Alex had returned to his flat in Dennistown, he was visited by Bob, who typically came round when he wanted to drink whisky and play CDs. Sitting in his kitchen, getting drunk and listening to the likes of Orange Juice and the Fire Engines, Alex showed Bob the bass and asked him,

'DO YOU WANT TO LEARN TO PLAY THE BASS THEN, BOB?'
'NO, I'M AN ARTIST, NOT A MUSICIAN.
'IT'S THE SAME THING.'
'OK THEN.'

This was essentially the conversation. However, at one in the morning, and after half a bottle of whisky, things allways seem simple. Bob was an artist, studying painting at the Glasgow School of Art, and the next day insisted he was now sober and rejected the case for an artist being the same as a musician. The two had a long philosophical debate about the essence of art until Alex made the point that 'art is just expression and there are many different ways to express yourself'. Bob relented – 'at least it'd be a giggle' – and took up the bass.

It was fitting for a band that would later profess to draw inspiration from the Dadaist art movement – which celebrated nonsense, travesty and incongruity – that one of its two founding members had never before touched the instrument he played.

Alex and Bob began to jam together in the former's Dennistown flat. **Lacking a drummer and a proper guitarist, however, they were fairly quiet.** After Franz Ferdinand became stars their Dennistown neighbours, Isabel and Thomas Johnston, were amazed that this rather quiet duo turned out to be the nucleus of Scotland's claim to rock fame.

'When he first moved in we realised he was in a band because we could hear them practising, they used to play up there all the time but there was no problem, they were not that noisy. We have other neighbours through the wall who like to throw a good party but they were quiet compared to that. Alex did actually come down to tell us what they were doing so that was really nice of him.'

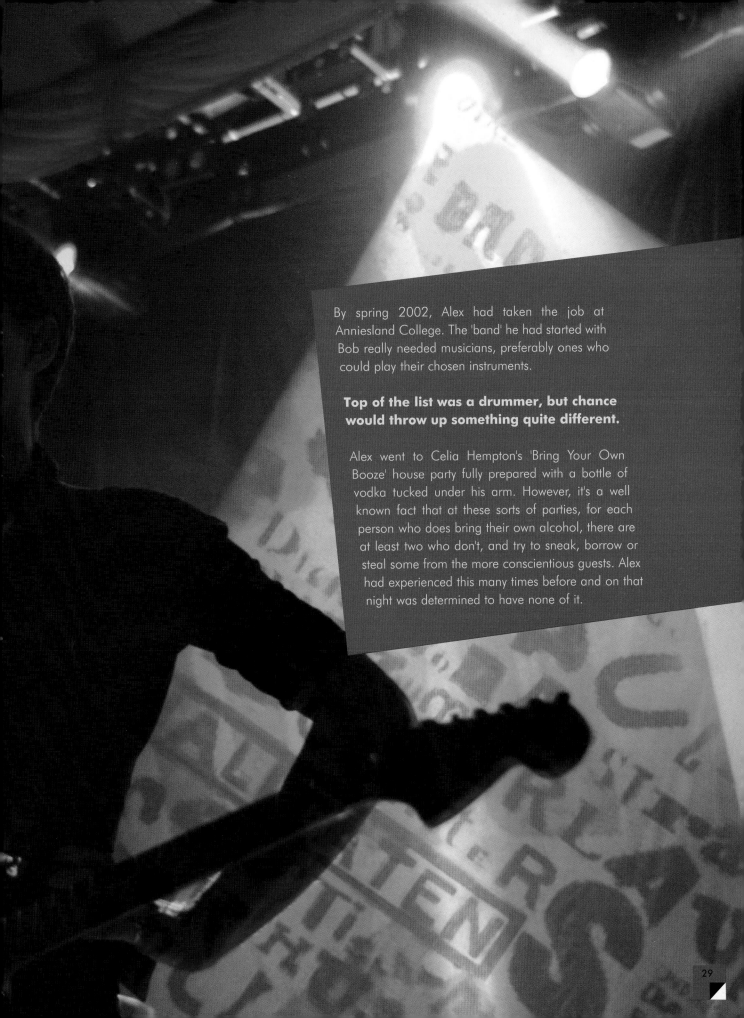

By spring 2002, Alex had taken the job at Anniesland College. The 'band' he had started with Bob really needed musicians, preferably ones who could play their chosen instruments.

Top of the list was a drummer, but chance would throw up something quite different.

Alex went to Celia Hempton's 'Bring Your Own Booze' house party fully prepared with a bottle of vodka tucked under his arm. However, it's a well known fact that at these sorts of parties, for each person who does bring their own alcohol, there are at least two who don't, and try to sneak, borrow or steal some from the more conscientious guests. Alex had experienced this many times before and on that night was determined to have none of it.

Unfortunately, he drank too much and left his bottle unattended; when he looked for it he saw 'this funny looking German guy at the other side of the room holding it'. Anywhere in the world this would be trouble but, in Glasgow, even though the issue was vodka not whisky, it was tantamount to razors at dawn.

This was avoided when the culprit attached to the bottle revealed under cross-examination that he was a black belt judo champion. Alex quickly decided the word is mightier than the sword and after a brief exchange the two realised that vodka was for cementing friendships not making enemies. All this was helped by the fact that as the culprit was a German and not an Englishman he wasn't familiar with the maxim of imperialism – possession is nine tenths of the law or its playground equivalent, finders-keepers.

However, it transpired after the vodka has been restored to its rightful owner that Nick had originally been born in England and only been brought up in Germany. Alex, although actually English himself with a Greek father, when faced with a Sassenach, even a German-reared one, always takes on a Scottish identity. With his moral high ground firmly established, he decided that the vodka-thief should at least do some community service. **Could he play drums? If he could then he could audition in Alex's band.**

Nick lied and said he could. In fact, he could not play drums but he could play virtually anything else. He was a Conservatory trained classical musician, who had played in a number of jazz groups. They decided to meet at Nick's South Side home.

Even in a social scene as bizarre as underground rock 'n' roll, Nick McCarthy stands out as an oddball. Born in Blackpool on December 1974 as Nicholas Augustine McCarthy, he moved with his family to a place he calls 'the drug-death capital of Germany' – Rosenheim, Bavaria.

This is where he spent most of his childhood, which left him with a slightly guttural English accent. This combined with his peculiar habit of dressing in Adam Ant style frillies did not endear him to your typical whisky-guzzling and fried-Mars-bar eating Scot. Alex says that Nick is 'slightly incongruous' but as his great uncle was the madcap comedian Jerry Lewis this, he thinks, may explain things.

He also lived next door to Franz Beckenbauer, the overlord of German football. Bob laughs, 'Nick has become a hero to us, because he kept nicking little mementoes from his house. **Honestly, it's nothing he'd miss, he hasn't stolen any football memorabilia. Well, Alex has got a pair of his trainers.** Not that they've made us any better at football…'

Although Nick describes himself as the strong man of the band: 'I am definitely the strongest… We have arm wrestling bouts and I'm definitely the champion. But in this band it's not very difficult to be the strongest.' This boast is rather deflated by what Alex discovered about Nick's judo training. It came to a premature end when he was 11 years old and a girl wiped the floor with him.

He went on to study as a classical pianist and double bassist at the Munich Conservatory – while he was there he also gained a reputation as a prodigious car-thief. Well, he didn't so much steal cars as borrow them for a while… rather like he had the vodka. 'His parents certainly named him well,' Alex reflects. Nick blames his *taking away and driving without the owner's consent* habit on the fact that, in his part of Germany, nobody seemed to lock their car doors. Another celebrated feat in his criminal career was when he and some friends broke into a supermarket and liberated the shelves of booze for a big student thrash.

At 27, Nick had just finished experimenting with the music scene in Germany, playing with progressive rock band Embryo for three years. Embryo constantly experimented with players and music: more than 300 musicians passed through the group during that three years and they played everything from jazz to ethnic folk. Nick, despite having a mainly jazz musical background, adapted to styles that he had not previously listened to, playing such instruments as bass, cello and Arabic lute. After leaving the group, he was in a kind of musical limbo.

His move to Glasgow was precipitated by his girlfriend Manuella coming over to study at the city's Art School. Nick talked about the idea of moving back to the U.K with a friend, who told him that Glasgow was a 'fun city' and the European City of Culture. This was all it took. When he was the object of Alex's citizen arrest, he had been there for just three months, searching fruitlessly for work.

Bob can remember seeing flyers put up around the college: 'Learn double bass! Learn guitar! Learn piano! Learn German! Phone Nick.' In spite of all this, Nick was still unemployed and was still spending his time cycling around town when he met Alex at Celia's.

While the fledgling band began jamming at Nick's place in Pollokshields, it soon became clear that the vodka thief was as truthful about his talent for percussion as he was about being a judo champion. On a borrowed drum kit, he played chaotically but just well enough to show he had some idea. As he later argued, the piano is actually a percussion instrument and in the past he'd dabbled at playing drums. But Alex and Bob knew that in the long run they'd have to pass on the idea of Nick playing drums.

Soon afterwards, Alex recruited his former drummer from Yummy Yur, Paul Thompson – the quartet for Franz was complete. However, Nick proved difficult about switching instruments and perversely insisted on being given time to develop his skills at the new instrument. Initially, then, Paul played guitar, which he could play well. This stopgap arrangement was also tolerated because Paul was at that time drumming with Pro Forma, which if he stayed there meant they would have to find someone else anyway.

Meanwhile, Paul discovered he rather like playing frontman guitar and sharing vocals, consequently by the time Nick threw in the towel on his drum-playing apprenticeship Paul did not want to sit behind the drums. There was also the slight problem that Nick had studied double-bass not guitar. Eventually, after the usual histrionics and compromises, common sense prevailed: Paul went behind the drums on the understanding that he still would get vocals and he could use low-rack toms. He objected to the way the high ones obscured the drummer from the audience. Alex said, 'In the interests of harmony in the band we had to concede greater visibility, so women will just have to continue to suffer such indecent exposure.'

By now a way of playing was germinating in Bob and Alex's heads:

'WE ALWAYS WANTED TO MAKE MUSIC THAT GIRLS COULD DANCE TO,' Bob explained, 'BECAUSE WE'D NOTICED A DISTINCT LACK OF GIRLS AT A LOT OF THE GIGS WE WENT TO. It was all men, standing around stroking their beards, there would be like one girl per ten men. So that was always in the back of our minds.'

The only thing left to do – aside that is from ensuring that people listened to them – was to choose a name for the band. Discussing this whiled away many fruitless hours, often as they watched daytime TV. The latter was very important for their zeitgeist and philosophy of life. It was during one of these appreciative sessions in front of the tube that Bob and Alex heard the name of a racehorse being announced on Channel 4's racing coverage – The Archduke.

As everyone knows, the sight of John McCririck tic-tacing away for his opinions is likely to overload even the racing enthusiast's attention span, so the two went off on an utterly irrelevant discussion about another Archduke, one whose death had proved to be the catalyst for the First World War.

'We started talking about Franz Ferdinand as a possible name. The whole history of the 20th century turned on that one moment in time. That appealed to us,' said Alex. 'It's a name everyone who has done standard grade history will know.'

For anyone who hasn't, Archduke Franz was heir to the throne of his uncle, Emperor Franz Joseph of Austria-Hungary, and while visiting Sarajevo on 28 June 1914, he and his wife were assassinated by a Serbian nationalist. Two hours before the Archduke arrived in Sarajevo twenty-two such conspirators were distributed over the whole route along which he had to travel. After one failed assassination attempt, the Archduke was persuaded to drive the shortest way out of the city.

His speeding car reached the bridge over the River Nilgacka where it was forced to slow down. Here another conspirator, Gavrilo Princip, lay in wait. As the car came abreast he drew his automatic pistol and fired two shots. The first struck the Archduchess in the abdomen. She was an expectant mother and died instantly. The second bullet struck the Archduke close to the heart, and he also died soon after. Austria-Hungary began sabre-rattling at Serbia, which triggered the start of World War I.

'We wanted a name which sounded good but which had implications of a grand event or a moment in history,' Alex explained. He began ticking off the requirements, "We'd like to usurp the name of Franz Ferdinand. When people hear that name, they won't think of some archduke whose death sparked the First World War - they'll think of this daft bunch of guys that met in Glasgow and formed a band.

IT'S A BIG ONE, BUT YOU'VE GOTTA HAVE DREAMS!'

Alex's wit was quick to get everyone to agree with the name in spite of it at best appearing idiosyncratic and at worst a mouthful of a white elephant. Alex would later justify it with an intellectual flourish:

'We chose Franz Ferdinand because it's literate, and it has a rhythm to it, and it just sounds good. Besides, the meaning gets removed so quickly from the original feeling. The Rolling Stones, Roxy Music – you don't think of the actual literal words, you think of the band.'

And then, with an ironic touch of hyperbole he added,

'PLUS, AFTER HIS ASSASSINATION, THE WHOLE WORLD CHANGED, AND NOTHING WAS EVER QUITE THE SAME.'

Word spread across the Glasgow music scene. The group was always going to be well known if only because of the involvement of Alex and Paul, who had for so long remained immovable fixtures in places such as the 13th Note. All of their musical CVs – apart from Bob's – were impeccable. On top of this, well established bands such as Belle & Sebastian played a large part in helping them get recognised.

In spite of all this, their first creditation came from a very different source, completely unconnected with the underground music scene. They were asked by the students of the Glasgow School of Art [GSA] to play at an exhibition called 'Girl Art'. The title of the exhibition suggested that the organisers had become confused as to the genders of the foursome but Alex dismissed that saying that it was all the posing Paul had done as a nude model. In fact, their credo of wanting to play music that girls would want to dance to had gone before them.

That the location for the Franz's first 'gig' was Celia Hempton's house in Sauchiehall Street — where Nick joyrided Alex's vodka — had a certain imprimatur from the gods. For Alex all that remained was to make a virtue of their not opening in a conventional venue: 'I think what attracted us to the artist end of the community in Glasgow was they had less pretensions and suppositions than the music crowd. I think that a lot of bands are stifled by the structure in which they have to play. They go through these three band showcases. You have to work your way up this ladder as if you're on a bloody apprenticeship. That's absolute bull shit.'

In Celia's bedroom lit by neon in front of a small crowd of friends on 3 May 2002 they opened with their now eponymous 'Take Me Out. Alex later claimed, **'There were only 40 people there. I was more scared than when I played live on TV to 40 million. It was about as raw as it can get. We had the crappiest selection of little amplifiers. It must have sounded NOT very professional, but exciting. It had a great atmosphere, off-the-cuff, like it just sort of happened.'**

The select few people who attended the party now have the pleasure of being able to say that they realised their potential first. Jacqueline Cameron — the inspiration for Jacqueline — is one who now proudly shows off the entry in her diary in which she predicted their stardom two years before it happened.

To prepare for the gig they practised sets in Nick's front room, playing to anyone they could get to listen, but soon realised the impracticality of this and began to search for another venue where they could both rehearse and perform their new songs to the public.

The Chateau long ago passed into the stuff of legends for all Franz Ferdinand fans. The band now uses the term to refer to any gig where they play with the revolutionary fervour that from the beginning was their mission statement.

In hindsight, Alex makes it sound as if they played it like a winning chess gambit:

'WHEN WE STARTED WE WANTED TO HAVE SOME CONTROL OVER OUR ENVIRONMENT.

'A LOT OF BANDS HAVE THE ENTHUSIASM KICKED OUT OF THEM BY PLAYING REALLY DREARY PUB VENUES THAT JUST CHURN BANDS THROUGH.'

The story of the original Chateau is not as legendary as Franz Ferdinand folklore has it but that doesn't detract from the way it highlights the band's origins.

It was situated in the part of Glasgow that used to be called the Gorbals, which was a byword for what the place was famous – vermin, poverty, crime and, most of all, violence. A tourist guide to the city will, if it even mentions the name, treat the Gorbals as some 19th century Glaswegian version of Dickensian London. But as any historian knows the slums of Glasgow were worse and lasted a lot longer than those of London. In fact, there are still remnants.

Alex and Nick went out hunting for an abandoned building in which they could play at Db levels that might ruin their own hearing but would not upset the neighbours. The two walked along the disused railway line that crosses over Paddy's market and the Clyde. They discovered two things: one, the line wasn't disused at all and, two, overlooking the Clyde River, a huge art-deco warehouse, which had obviously been boarded up for years, that might well suit their purposes.

Totally enamoured with the strangeness and relative (for the centre of Glasgow) remoteness of the location, the band got in touch with the owner of the warehouse, who had long since given up on using it for anything, and allowed the band to rent out the sixth floor. Crystallising their feelings of romance and revolution, Franz Ferdinand christened the venue 'The Chateau'.

Alex now says: **'The legendary status of The Chateau baffles us in a way. We wanted to do something different and we wanted to have fun. Someone had told us you could get round the 'no bar' by raffling drinks rather than selling drinks. That's what we did. And Franz Ferdinand played.'** It helped that they hooked up the electricity supply, too.

At one point in its long history, the warehouse had stored sports equipment. The group at first held a Sports and Leisure night: rowing machines strapped to trolleys were raced, vibra-belts wobbled, weights were lifted and rifles were shot from the saddle of a rocking horse.

The second Chateau event was grander and more arty. On the fifth floor, artist Robb Mitchell and moving gallery Switchspace gathered together a collection of artists to put on an exhibition which focused on social interaction. One installation was entitled 'Social Whirls' and consisted of 28 independently revolveable, circular floor panels. It was the sort of exhibit that wins Whitbread Prizes and rockets the blood pressure of the taxpayers of Tunbridge Wells.

On the sixth floor, Ferdinand brought together some of the best music in Glasgow, boasting performances from rock bands Uncle John and Whitelock, Park Attack and jazz group Scatter.

Lighting was in the form of a bank of sun beds that had been found on one of the floors, which were wired to flicker on and off randomly as the bands played.

THE SET WAS ENTITLED FREAK SHOW, THE VENUE'S WEBSITE BLURBED AS:
'FRANZ FERDINAND: ASSASSINATION BY BLACK HAND – MEMBERS OF PRO FORMA, KARELIA, AND THE YUMMY FUR IN JERKY RENDITION OF KRAUT DISCO LIVE TRANSMISSIONS, YOU KNOW, KIND OF SEXY IN A SKINNY WAY.'

The Chateau events encapsulated everything fun about rock and roll. Although the average age of those attending was about twenty-five, the spirit was that of a bunch of sixteen-year-olds playing at a school rock concert, and feeling like rebels because they swore on stage.

Unfortunately, rebellion as a grown up is slightly more complex. As more and more people began to arrive, the police were alerted and closed down the event, attempting to make arrests on the charges of running an illegal bar and contravening various health and safety, fire hazard and noise abatement regulations.

The official Franz Ferdinand website recalled the events: **'It felt liberating. Then the police arrived. They seemed terrified.** There were only a few of them and they were panicking. Very soon another couple of vanloads arrived. It was like a scene from a speakeasy in prohibition-era Chicago. As the cops were racing up one staircase, crates of booze were flying down the other.'

Alex was the only member of the band to be arrested, which the Franz Ferdinand website faithfully records: 'When Alex was chatting to the cops over a cup of tea down the cells – everyone friends again – they said that they had been looking for the place for a month. They had been driving round the block, trying to find a way into where the noise was coming from. It seemed that they were just happy to be confused no longer.'

The charges against Alex were quickly dropped. Now any event at the Chateau was a sell-out, some of which even a few cops attended... well those in the drug squad. Alex had been very keen to tell them about Bob's dad being a serving police officer with the West Yorkshire Constabulary, which secured them much more of a licence than they legally warranted but still less than they needed.

The group started again to look around for venues at which they could play to their growing number of fans. The successful Glaswegian artist Lucy McKenzie proved sympathetic to their cause and encouraged them to play at her Flourish Studios. Together, they organised similar exhibitions to those put on at the Chateau, calling them the 'Flourish Nights'. Stereo – a bar in the city – also backed them, letting them gig there. Meanwhile the band could still put shows on at The Chateau until another base, equally magnificent, was found. On Tobago Street there is a Victorian courtroom and gaol which, until Nick McCarthy discovered it, had been abandoned for over 30 years.

'I WAS CYCLING AROUND ONE DAY AND I SAW WHAT LOOKED LIKE A BIG HOUSE, McCarthy recalled. 'IT WAS OPEN, SO I WENT INTO THE BACK YARD AND FOUND IT WAS A JAIL. INSIDE THERE WAS A CELL BLOCK ON TWO FLOORS, WOODEN DOORS AND FUNCTIONING LOCKS, ALL DATING FROM AROUND 1850. THERE WAS A MASSIVE COURTROOM AS WELL. IT WAS ALL THERE.'

The band took over the Bridgetown Jail and christened it 'The Chateau' as well. For one night on 15 February 2003 they staged a Franz Ferdinand extravaganza.

All the cells were used to exhibit local artists - it was called **'Cells Out'** – with special attention being given to the works of 'some guy called Will' – the graffiti scored on a cell wall by one Willie Whitelaw, dated 1888.

The courtroom was converted into a stage replete with a sound system, assembled from speakers and amps that were borrowed from fellow musicians, that would have done for a stadium rock concert.

ON THE NIGHT, IT WAS COLDER IN THE BUILDING THAN OUTSIDE, BUT THE FANS DIDN'T FEEL THE COLD – FRANZ FERDINAND WAS BLAZING.

The band were on an 'underground' roll. There was a buzz about Franz Ferdinand – not just in Glasgow but across the UK. This was a rock band that played music with style, poetry and wit – music you could dance to and you could learn from, too. The makers and shakers on the street had singled out Franz Ferdinand as a test of whether or not you were cool.

The band didn't know this, of course, but they realised that something was happening. The problem was what, and how they make money from it? They started using cell A9 in Bridgetown Jail as a base for writing, rehearsing and brainstorming about how they could improve their act as well as well as their finances.

One obvious move was to produce an album but there was also their art school following. They put on a gig at the Glasgow School of Art in April 2003 that was more about saying thank you to their hardcore fans than anything else.

Alex remembers, 'We were just expecting it to be another gig at the art school, then we saw the guest list and there were about forty labels on it. There was a guy holding up a mobile phone to the stage while we were playing. We arranged to meet some of these guys and it felt like some daft *Carry On* film, or a Terry and June episode. You had to keep them separate. **They were all giving each other dirty looks. One asked us to sign on the night and I never thought that would happen**.'

Smitten with the band's electric disco-laced garage, the record companies tried sign them up with telephone number record deals and the usual 'helicopter rides'[oil companies use them to impress the local peasants] like expensive restaurants, limo rides and lines of coke.

THE BAND MEMBERS ATE THE FOOD, ENJOYED THE RIDES, HOOVERED UP THE COKE, THEN FLATLY REFUSED ANY DEAL ON OFFER.

Instead, in May 2003, the band signed to Lawrence Bell's small but respected independent label, Domino. Their choice Alex attributes to Bell's 'real enthusiasm and genuine love for music'; a passion he backed with the personal touch, 'Lawrence had a totally different attitude from all the other labels. He never said he'd buy us some big fancy meal – he cooked us dinner instead. We liked him and we liked his ideals.'

One can only imagine the group's confusion at this stage – at one moment they were a mildly successful Glasgow band, playing for art school students and other self-proclaimed 'ponces' in friends' bedrooms, abandoned ware-houses and mothballed jails, the next they were being booked to play at some of the biggest festivals in the country.

This was to a great extent a result of the amount of faith Lawrence Bell had in them. Asked in an interview with www.incendiarymag.com in September 2003 what the next big Domino band would be, he plugged Franz Ferdinand over the likes of The Kills and Radiohead's favoured one-man band, Four Tet.

He replied, **'We've just signed a band called Franz Ferdinand from Glasgow; I think they're going to do really well. They're like a sorta pop rock/early Joseph Cane art school band. They've got great songs and they're very colourful and fresh, so I've got high hopes for them.'**

This was not to mention the fact that they were already well on the way to recording their first single. The band had travelled down to London for the day, with Alex calling in sick at the Anniesland college and Bob skiving off art school. The song they chose to record was the catchy 'Darts of Pleasure'.

Alex recalled, 'We went to London on the train; we couldn't take all of our gear, so we just phoned up friends there and borrowed amps and drum kits and stuff. I pulled a sickie and then bumped into one of my colleagues on the train. I was teaching at Anniesland College at the time, there was a big free period coming up and I thought I'd chance it.'

Paul chimed in, 'NICK WAS WORKING AS A GUITAR TEACHER AND BOB HAD NEVER REALLY HAD A JOB. I HAD AN ASSESSMENT FOR MY DEGREE SHOW AND WE HAD TO RECORD THE SINGLE AT THE SAME TIME. IT WAS CRAZY.

'I MISSED WEEKS OF ART SCHOOL, BUT I GOT AWAY WITH IT.'

Paul was awarded his doctorate.

In June, they played their first major gig back in Glasgow at The Barrowland venue. The band supported Pete Doherty's Libertines. Alex was confident that Franz Ferdinand would soon eclipse groups like The Libertines. Watching them made him determined never to let his group become engulfed in the kind of druggie chaos that Doherty generated.

'The Barrowland was just surreal. It was the first proper big show we'd done,' Bob said.

Alex added, 'It felt like we were stepping into someone else's world in a way. All these guys lifting your gear for you — what's that about?'

They went on to play at Scotland's premier music festival — Balado's 'T in the Park' in July as an 'up and coming' act supporting globally acclaimed bands such as Coldplay, The Darkness and the legendary R.E.M.

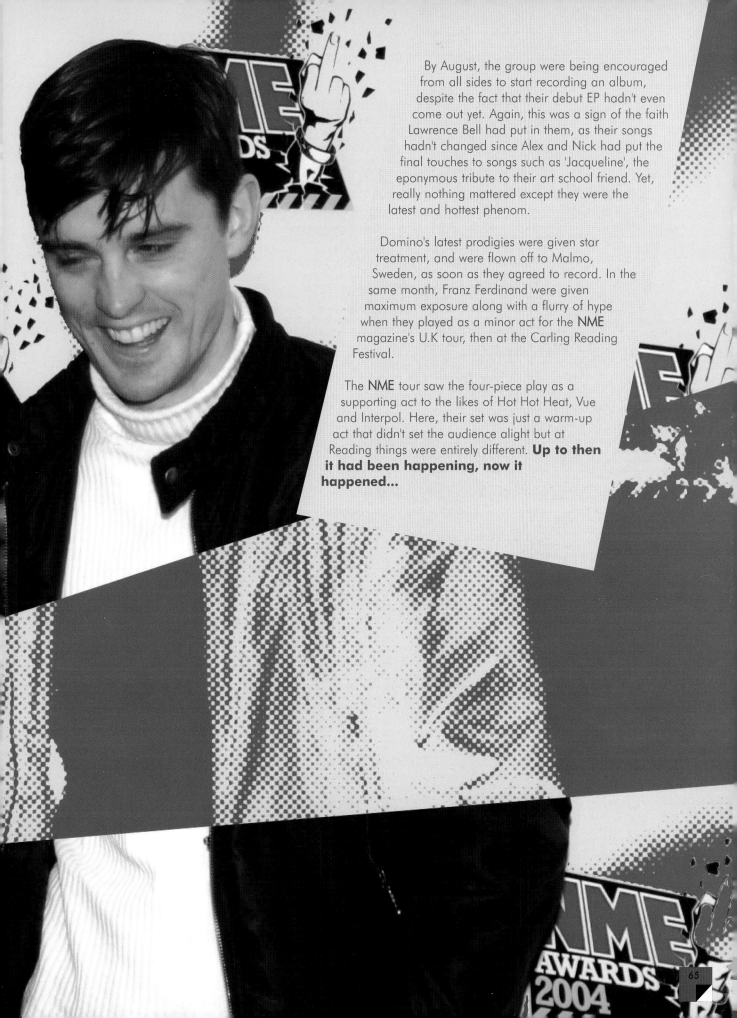

By August, the group were being encouraged from all sides to start recording an album, despite the fact that their debut EP hadn't even come out yet. Again, this was a sign of the faith Lawrence Bell had put in them, as their songs hadn't changed since Alex and Nick had put the final touches to songs such as 'Jacqueline', the eponymous tribute to their art school friend. Yet, really nothing mattered except they were the latest and hottest phenom.

Domino's latest prodigies were given star treatment, and were flown off to Malmo, Sweden, as soon as they agreed to record. In the same month, Franz Ferdinand were given maximum exposure along with a flurry of hype when they played as a minor act for the **NME** magazine's U.K tour, then at the Carling Reading Festival.

The **NME** tour saw the four-piece play as a supporting act to the likes of Hot Hot Heat, Vue and Interpol. Here, their set was just a warm-up act that didn't set the audience alight but at Reading things were entirely different. **Up to then it had been happening, now it happened...**

Franz played on the Carling stage alongside bands such as Razorlight and Keane, who ascended to similar fame at around the same time as Franz Ferdinand themselves.

It was just two o'clock when Alex came on stage and said, as he is won't to, '**I am the new Scottish gentry**,' the crowd just erupted in excitement. This was the band they wanted to hear.

They ripped into 'Take Me Out'.

So if you're lonely
You know I'm here waiting for you
I'm just a crosshair
I'm just a shot away from you
And if you leave here
You leave me broken, shattered, I lie
I'm just a crosshair
I'm just a shot, then we can die

Alex was astonished at the reception they received: 'You could tell there was some sort of buzz. We were playing in a tent and it was crammed, and the single wasn't even out yet.'

As **Dot Music** remarked afterwards: 'With their thermometer currently as hot as Jay Z armed with MDMA goggles, eyeing Beyonce's almost illegal booty in cut-down denims, the word is out on this Glaswegian four-piece. Indeed, Dot Music finds itself in an almost partisan tent, buzzing with… anticipation.'

While the magazine made an effort to keep their feet on the ground rather than prostrate themselves in homage, nonetheless it confessed that when Alex sung 'I know you will surrender' [Darts of Pleasure] they were already on their knees. The review retained a cloak of respectability by pointing out 'Franz Ferdinand do little new and are surfing on the New Wave 20 years too late.' If Franz Ferdinand were 20 years too late, then they have pioneered time travel.

Darts of Pleasure was in fact released as an EP in the U.K on the 8th September, with the distinctive cover art designed by Paul who, according to Alex had 'too much time on his hands, and got over excited with the felt tips'. It contained four tracks: 'Darts of Pleasure', 'Van Tango', 'Shopping for Blood', 'Tell Her Tonight'. Two of the tracks were home demos and, in all, the running time of the four was a little under 16 minutes.

'Darts of Pleasure' was the benchmark. Alex said, 'This was the song people were humming after gigs. That's been our criterion for a lot of the songs that we've chosen.'

The hum-along quality 'Darts of Pleasure' is also enhanced by another Franz Ferdinand trademark, sensuality. This is not a boyband that shags groupies, it is group that makes love to their ladies. The lyrics are intelligent and cleverly rhymed, with the essence of the ballad being distilled in the lines:

Skin can feel my lips they tingle – tense anticipation
This one is an easy one, feel the word and melt upon it

Alex's crooning emphasises the meaning of the song – the fact that simple words spoken artfully can be the 'best way of seducing anyone', as he said in an interview with NME magazine. Not to renege on their status as intellectual art-rockers, however, 'Darts' even includes a not-so-subtle reference to the Shakespearian metaphor for an orgasm – a death, contained in the lines:

Words of poisoned darts of pleasure
Died... and so you died

Rather different from the lines in German at the end of the song:

ICH HEISSE SUPERFANTASTISCH!
ICH TRINKE SCHAMPUS MIT LACHSFISCH!
ICH HEISSE SU-PER-FAN-TAS-TISCHI

Nick, the inspiration behind the climactic chorus due to his German upbringing, said at Yahoo's Launch: 'What we're saying in German means, "I'm called Super-Fantastic". Which is just a ridiculous joke; the next line means, uh, "I drink champagne with smoked salmon". It's just like this big New Year's Eve kind of thing at the end, ridiculing it a bit.'

Of course I like it, but it's only rock 'n' roll, after all. Franz Ferdinand have the artifice to suspend the audience's reality as it gives itself up to the song, then the wit to bring it back to earth with a send-up.

Franz Ferdinand's debut EP was greeted with much praise by the music press, music industry and media critics in general. In much the same words as the title bestowed upon another British band that became popular at around the same time, The Darkness, Franz Ferdinand were acclaimed as 'the saviours of rock and roll'. John Peel gave them airtime on his late night Radio 1 show. The buying public, though, were unimpressed, with sales stagnating shortly after release.

This incited a lot of comment on the internet, with one in particular making the right connection:

'DARTS OF PLEASURE' CLEARLY DEMONSTRATES THAT, THOUGH THE EP ON THE WHOLE IS NOTEWORTHY BUT NOT EXTRAORDINARY, FRANZ FERDINAND HAS SOME SERIOUS POTENTIAL –

AND PERHAPS THIS IS THE SOURCE OF THE MAMMOTH HYPE FOR THESE SCOTS.'

Another feature of the band is that from the beginning it provoked more internet traffic than virtually any other emerging rock 'n' roll group. Perhaps Bob's reaction to the disappointment explains the interest. He said that he 'wanted the band to convey the raw emotion of Field Marshal Haig's tears as he read the casualty reports from the front.'

Franz Ferdinand's constituency is the Blackadder generation: the intelligent, smart, humorously ironical, successful, wired counter-culture.

To mark their failure to break into the charts, Franz Ferdinand launched a quirky arty video to go with the single. Nick told Yahoo's Launch: **'The filming was out of Alex's mouth. He actually has a false tooth, and they took that out and put a miniature camera inside it.'**

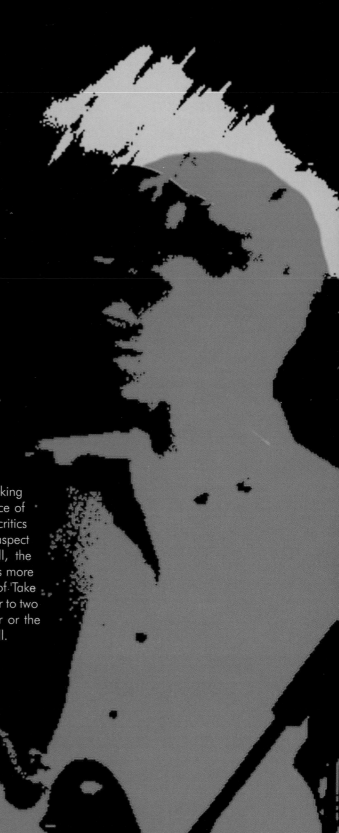

The release of *Darts* didn't inhibit their heavy touring schedule during the latter months of 2003. Throughout September they continued to put on gigs in Scotland, England and even went as far as Berlin to play at the Röter Salon alongside Husky Stash. October saw them break free of their supporting role as they launched their first headline tour with The Ludes.

Alex commented later: 'It was good to do a headline tour at that point, rather than playing in someone else's shadow. I still have this attitude that playing gigs is what I do when I take time off from my crap job so, in a way, I can't believe I get to do it all the time.'

One of these gigs was a performance to mark the 10th anniversary of Domino Records at the Electrowerkz, London (24 October 2003). Fittingly for a dank bank alley in Islington, the gig was given the title of 'The Chateau' in an attempt to return to the DIY atmosphere which was a leitmotif of their early Glasgow gig

FRANZ FERDINAND WERE DELAYED AND, FOR ONCE, WERE LATE STARTING THEIR SET. ALEX ALWAYS PRIDED HIMSELF ON RESPECTING THE AUDIENCE: 'I CAN'T STAND IT WHEN YOU SEE BANDS AND IT LOOKS LIKE THEY'VE HAD TO DRAG THEMSELVES UP TO GET ONSTAGE. IF YOU DON'T WANT TO BE THERE, GET OFF THE BLOODY STAGE.'

They took the opportunity to amuse people with a talking army truck outside the venue itself. This offbeat piece of entertainment served to highlight a fact that many critics were beginning to pick up on – a certain military aspect to the fun-loving group of art students. After all, the band's name spells it out. All of their album art has more than of an element of propaganda in it. The lyrics of 'Take Me Out' are left ambivalent as to whether they refer to two people exchanging glances across a dance floor or the tortured thoughts of a sniper moving in for the kill.

On top of this, their performances are organised in a sharp, military fashion. Alex, for example, lays down strict guidelines on how the band should sound and be presented. Rules include no guitar or drum solos, no chords (just notes) and looking the audience straight in the eye. They do not 'perform' so much as 'show' their themselves and their music.

There are many who could see the music industry as an army that, like all armies, must have its officers and its squaddies. Where groups like Oasis, whose front man Noel Gallagher famously declared in 2005 that he had only read one book in his life, are very much drawn from the other ranks, Franz Ferdinand are definitively officer class. They read, they think and, whether they talk or write lyrics or compose songs or make videos, it shows.

In spite of this, they do not pull rank. They don't ask to be credited for being branded as the 'smart man's band'. Literary or arty references do not sell records. 'To me, there's nothing worse than singing about "that book by Nabokov" in your song,' says Kapranos, instancing the song by Sting and the Police, 'Don't stand so Close to Me'.

The Franz Ferdinand formula has been to evolve a style that strikes a chord with the public, play hum-along music that celebrates having a good time.

MISERY AND ANGST WORKED BY PUBLIC SCHOOL BED-WETTERS SUCH AS COLDPLAY AND KEANE HAS ITS FANS BUT FRANZ DO FEEL-GOOD.

The Electrowerkz gig emphasised the band's arty image. Ben Bollig, from **No Ripcord** magazine wrote a canny article that pinned down the FF appeal: 'The term "gig" no longer applies. As the thin divides between music, performance, art, installation and video are progressively transgressed and reworked, it is artists (performers? stars?) like the four-headed Arch Duke who are at the forefront of the third millennium's gestamptkunstwerk. Wagner would be proud.'

'In the years since 2001, FF have taken the Chateau blueprint — artists, music, DJ, booze, rampant disregard for city bylaws and health and safety — and created one of the most dynamic art spectacles of Glasgow, a place where creative rules are broken and great pop occurs.

'There's a charmingly found or readymade feel about tonight's affair, especially as the masses bounce up to the main room along a corridor lined with fluorescent paint, installed and faintly subversive art, and the kind of rickety stairs that will challenge even the most well-healed smurf boot.

'Where they really win over the soon pumping crowd is in their concentrated energy, bouncing round the stage like well-dressed ping-pong balls and holding the tightest of arrangements and harmonies. There's even a falsetto and pure pop key changes to cement their appeal.

'REINVENTING THE WHEEL ANYONE?'

Bollig's take on Franz Ferdinand reminds us that their casting is nothing new. The four man band featuring tortured singer, psycho guitarist, laconic bass player and an animal on the drums had already been proven to great effect, and has drawn numerous comparisons between the Franz and the likes of other hit indie rockers such as New York's The Strokes or English punk band, Joy Division.

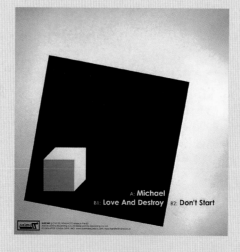

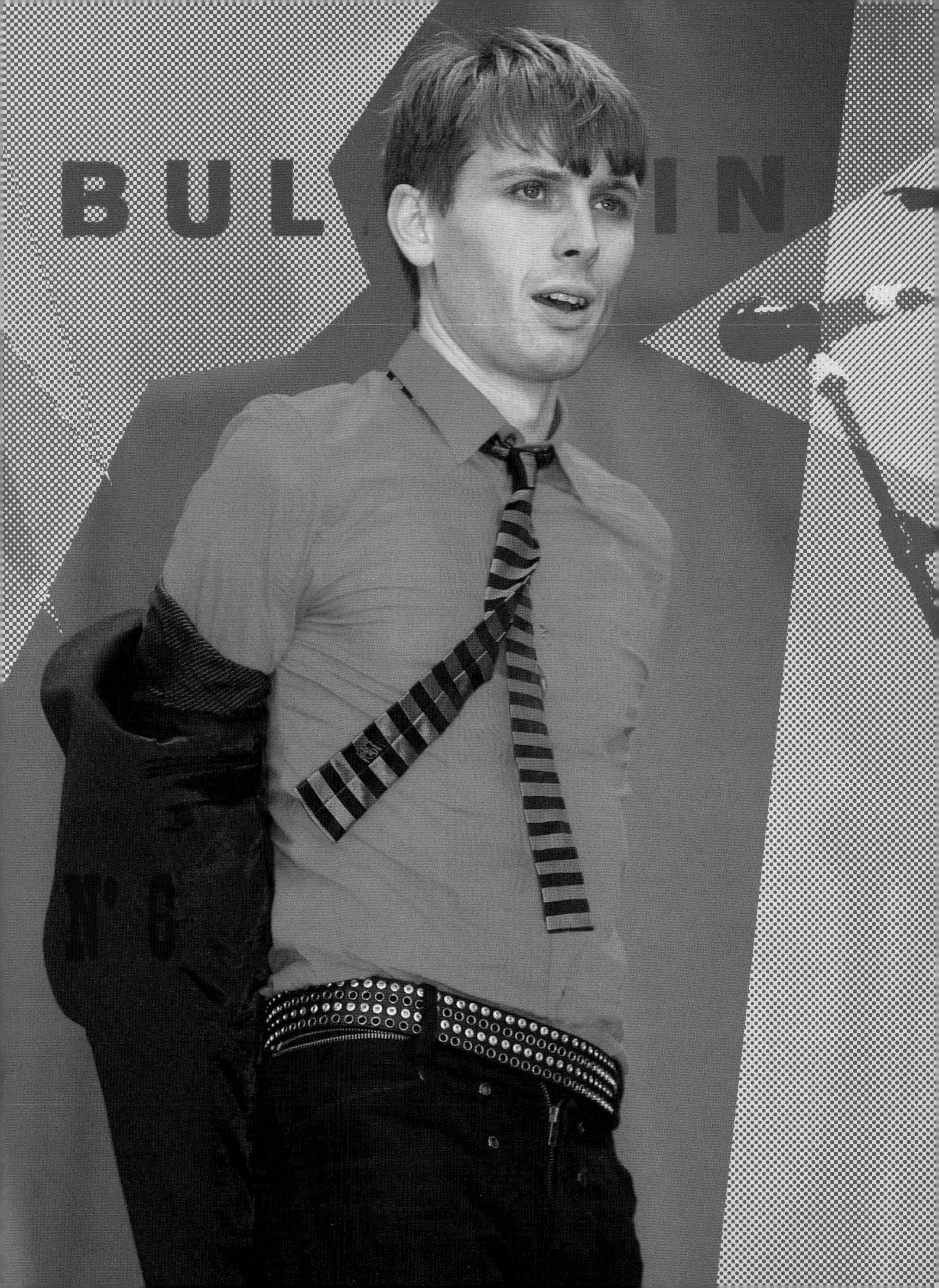
BUL
IN
N°6

Another gig in October was also part of their tour with The Ludes and was played at the Cambridge boat race. **X-Ray** magazine, part of the XFM radio station corporation, reviewed the 'energetic' performance:

'Barely 30-odd gigs into their career, their performance oozes enthusiastic confidence. Rhythm section Bob Hardy and Paul Thomson provide a funktastic twist and turn backbone, channelled with telepathic understanding. In Kapranos and Nick McCarthy, they've got two mesmerising frontmen for the price of one – the former, brooding with a Mark E Smith style "delivery-ah", the livewire latter all Kevin Rowland-esque yelps and loving-it grins.

'With a ten song set that hints at a debut album of soaring, guitar-pop greatness, their youthful energy and theatrical razzle mean the mosh-pit's unfamiliarity with most tracks is bypassed. The audience can't help but move to the infectious 'Sound and Vision' groove and vocal interplay of 'Tell Her Tonight... Then comes the punk-funk of superb forthcoming single "Take Me Out" – proof this is a band that prefers the joyful pop of Chic to the hip-swaying cool of ESG.'

November saw the band make their TV debut on Later with Jools Holland in Oxford. Alex described the experience as being '...nerve-wracking. You start playing and all these television cameras zoom in at you like formation jet fighters zooming in for the kill. As we were playing, I remember glancing across at the studio and Annie Lennox was dancing along again. It was thoroughly bizarre. We hope people can see what we have done and think that if four dafties like us can do it, they can do it too.'

Bizarre it may have been, but the Franz put on a set which won them instant acclaim from all sides. The official reviewer for the BBC got it:

'FRANZ FERDINAND – STUPID NAME, INTERESTING POSES AND DODGY HAIRCUTS... OH AND "GARAGE-PUNK" MUSIC TO DIE FOR.'

They *had* invented the wheel.

Franz's TV debut on 'Later...' in November did much to establish their credibility as a truly impressive new band, rather than just an over-hyped pipe dream. It proved to any remaining doubters that they could produce a scintillating live performance as well as lay down great tracks on records. They quickly embarked on a tour around Europe to capitalise on this success and to promote the sale of *Darts*, which by now was picking up due to the wave of publicity they were receiving.

The group also managed to cross the Atlantic, knowing full well that this is a perilous journey for British stars attempting to sell themselves to an American public already choking on their glut of home-grown talent. This was especially true of New York, home turf of The Strokes, but Franz Ferdinand managed to establish themselves as a supporting act in three of New York's clubhouse venues – The Coral, Piano and The Mercury Lounge. This was when Alex of dapper Franz met Eleanor from the Fiery Furnaces for the first time.

The Fiery Furnaces are an eccentric four-piece blues/indie rock band heralding again from New York. The mainstay of the group is sibling duo Matt and Eleanor Friedberger. This is not a joke, the family have German roots. Franz Ferdinand immediately credited the Furnaces' idiosyncratic style of music and original song writing, and agreed to play more gigs with them in the future.

December began in much the same way as November had ended – with constant touring. This time, however, the atmosphere was relaxed not hectic as Franz played as a supporting act for their old friends and role models, Belle & Sebastian.

'Belle & Sebastian are the perfect example of a band who keep it enjoyable,' Alex declared. 'They never talk about it as if it's a job and that's a really essential thing for any band to retain. The show they played in Liverpool, the atmosphere was astonishing. It was this old theatre, and Nick and I gatecrashed this guy's box, took a bunch of flowers and chucked them on to the stage. I'm pretty certain we couldn't hurt the band with a bunch of flowers, but the bouncers threw us out.'

After a lengthy tour of Britain with the group, playing at venues such as London's Astoria, Franz ended the year with a short trip to play in Barcelona. Another gig but a short break, too, in one of the true art capitals of the world. Their next gig was Edinburgh's famous Hogmanay festival for 2004.

Unfortunately for the 100,00 revellers in Prince Street, the heavens really did open up and the concert had to be cancelled. The band re-convened with 50 or so determined party-goers in a friend's flat. Fifteen minutes into the New Year, they opened with a 'gloriously ramshackle' version of 'Cheating on You'.

Alex remembered, 'It was the perfect New Year, full of ups and downs. We felt elated that we were playing Princes Street Gardens in front of all these people. When it was cancelled we were all standing round thinking, "What now?" There was this flurry of excitement as we phoned people up and tried to work out something to do before the bells. It was like *Challenge Anneka!* It also brought back the spirit we had at the beginning, doing things on our own terms.'

In mid-January, they released their second EP, four weeks before the official unveiling of their debut album. 'Take Me Out' is the third track of the EP of the same name. Featuring ripping guitar riffs and, once again, brilliantly colour-coded art work on the record sleeve, 'Der-der-diddle-ur-dur-dur' became the first signature tune of the year.

As well as being humalong *heavy*, 'Take Me Out' has lyrics that work on different levels, so those of a more intellectual disposition can get off on analysing what they really mean.

So if you're lonely,
You know I'm here waiting for you,
I'm just a crosshair,
I'm just a shot away from you

The lyrics could well be a metaphor for two people exchanging glances across a dance floor. Just as easily, however, they could be could be a straightforward reference to the thoughts of two snipers, each trying to catch the other out. The latter reading brings to mind scenes from Jude Law's Hollywood blockbuster, *Enemy at the Gates*, which was released at around the same time as Alex and Nick first started to co-operate with their song writing in 2001.

Alex, however, was as always quick to crush any idea that the band were working on an intellectual basis first and foremost. Just because their lyrics were cleverly ambivalent, their main priority, as he kept repeating, was to make catchy songs that girls, or indeed boys could dance to.

Bob interjected 'It is a unisex appeal.

'THE MUSIC WE HATE IS THAT OF EARNEST BOYS MAKING COMPLICATED MUSIC FOR OTHER

EARNEST BOYS.
'THERE'S NOTHING FINER THAN SEEING PEOPLE DANCE TO YOUR SONG; SO WE DO MUSIC EASY TO DANCE TO.'

Alex later used an anecdote to describe the sound Franz Ferdinand were aiming for: 'To me, pop music is music that moves you without engaging the brain; and then allows you to engage the brain afterwards. You dance and you feel the passion, and then you can sort through the grander ideas which the music suggests.

'A friend of mine said that he'd been playing our album and his three-year-old daughter was dancing around the room, singing along, making up her own words, jumping around and stuff. To me, that is fantastic. That's the best indication that we've done something right.

'A THREE-YEAR-OLD DOESN'T INTELLECTUALISE MUSIC, DOESN'T HEAR IT WITHIN ANY SOCIAL CONTEXTS, AND HAS NO IDEA WHAT'S COOL AND WHAT'S NOT COOL.

'ALL A THREE-YEAR-OLD KNOWS IS "THIS IS FUN TO DANCE AROUND TO" AND "I LIKE THE TUNE". THAT'S WHAT MUSIC SHOULD BE – THAT'S THE ESSENCE.'

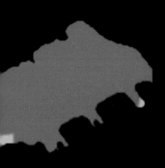

The *Top of the Pops* of his day, however, was dominated by rock bands not bubble-gum pop aimed at the pre-teen market. Alex shrugged: 'To be honest, mainstream pop music just passes over my head. I ignore most of the stuff on *Top of the Pops* and Radio 1. The problem is, it's bland, bland, bland. It's retrogressive. There's nothing progressive in it at all.

'It makes kids think that to get anywhere they have to have a team of stylists and a Simon Cowell to tell them whether they're any good. It discourages people from creating for themselves. They think they need this big machine behind them. That's bullshit – that's where the worst pop music comes from. The thing is, being in a band is simple. People seem to forget that. And fun."

Top of the Pops was no coincidence. The well-planned release of 'Take Me Out' had paid enormous dividends as it strutted into the charts at number 3. After *Darts* had failed to breach the Top 40 last September, their strategy for 2004 was simple and, in part, boy band-esque. A clever press strategy convinced the NME, a magazine that likes to think it is pretty good at spotting the next big thing, that Franz Ferdinand were, yes, the next big thing.

Then came 'Take Me Out', a single made for radio – still the most effective medium for selling records – at the very moment that radio was starting to wonder what all the fuss was about. Guns cocked, Franz Ferdinand really went to work. The week before the release, as press and radio frothed at the mouth, they played concerts at record shops, followed by signing sessions.

These appearances then became 'events', using the 'Chateau' strategy, generating yet more press and yet more radio play.

It was at this junction that Franz Ferdinand began to learn the price of universal acclaim. As an indie rock band, this very thing, combined with the amount of hype they were receiving, could well have led to a disaster. The NME magazine, normally fairly even-handed, illustrated this phenomenon when it reviewed a gig at the Birmingham Academy on 27th January:

'FRANZ FERDINAND ARE SO HOT RIGHT NOW IT HURTS. INDEED, IT'S SO HOT IN THE ACADEMY THAT BY THE TIME FF FLOUNCE ON STAGE SEVERAL YELPING BOYS AND GIRLS ARE MOIST WITH EXCITEMENT.

'FF give us a pop-tastic "Take Me Out", a throbbing "Darts Of Pleasure", and a song about boy-sex called "Michael". To some, FF are fucking brilliant, to others, especially the Funeral for a Friend fans hanging off the balcony and throwing beer at the punters below, FF are fucking awful.'

The review was in reference to a gig the boys played as part of NME's annual tour of new bands. They were given pride of place over and above the likes of the Von Bondies, Funeral for a Friend and The Rapture. On top of this they were given the accolade of 'the band that will change your life' by the magazine.

'It's strange reading that sort of stuff and we tend to distance ourselves from it.' Alex claimed.

'We take the Woody Allen approach to reviews to be honest – we try not to read them. We write music, and we play music, and we record music and we do that from our own frame of reference, and it's fantastic to stick it out to the world and for people to appreciate it, or not to appreciate it.'

Much as they seem to insist that they are only interested in making people 'appreciate their music', Franz Ferdinand rely on their image more than most pop bands. Their attempts to deny it only highlight their shrewd sense of self-promotion in playing to both sides of the coin. On one day, they would claim that they wanted the music to speak for itself, that they didn't read their own reviews. But on most days, rather than shun the press like any right-on indie punk band should, they would make 'on-message' statements to journalists that were bound to result in flattering coverage. For example:

'It's refreshing to find a band who would rather discuss the influence Russian Constructivist art has on their record covers than what's on their stereo. Furthermore, they understand that giving interviews is a vital part of the wider picture, as is the artwork and the videos and the haircuts and the shoes and the on-stage theatrics. It's all a part of conveying the message.' [The Guardian]

The 'Chateau' image that they had acquired quite naturally was proving to be a double edged sword. The band had two choices — either they surrender themselves to a cult indie status, which was ready-made for them, or they could try for the big time. It was Hobson's choice, really, and Alex was adamant:

'WE'RE REALLY ANTI-ELITIST AS A BAND. I HATE THE CLIQUEYNESS OF THE SCENE; IT HAPPENS A LOT WITHIN INDIE. LIKE, A BAND IS ONLY COOL WHEN THEY'RE ONLY LIKED BY A SMALL SECTION OF SOCIETY, AND IT'S SUCH A LOAD OF BOLLOCKS.'

Right at this pivotal point in their history, *Franz Ferdinand* was released on the 9th February 2004.

Franz Ferdinand was a remarkable success, reaching number 3 in the UK charts and 32 in America. Significantly, it was to stay in Billboard's top 200 for over a year.

One reviewer wrote:'***Franz Ferdinand* is an unrelentingly smart, fluffy, and fun debut.** This Scottish four-piece plays vaguely angular, guitar-heavy post-punk that makes you want to dance around the room while playing air guitar. It's the ideal hipster guilty-pleasure music.

'THIS IS WHAT THE RAPTURE AND INTERPOL WOULD SOUND LIKE IF THEY WROTE SONGS HALF AS GOOD AS THOSE THEY RIP OFF, OR THE STROKES IF THEIR PARENTS HAD SENT THEM TO ART SCHOOL INSTEAD OF THE FASHION ACADEMY.'

The surprises on the album were easily the tracks 'Auf Achse' and 'Dark of the Matinee'. The first showed that the band were as capable of producing songs of a darker nature as well as just 'fluffy' pop. It has an unsettling aggression underneath its romantic yearning, its cheap synthesised strings and pianos underscoring its low-rent moodiness and ruined glamour.

It caused widespread amusement when the band were conducting a live interview, and one fan mistook the word 'boy' for 'Bob', asking what the lyrics *She's not so special so/ look what you've done, Bob*' were supposed to signify. Had Bob been up to something naughty that the band didn't like and the fans didn't know about?

ALEX HARDLY HELPED. 'MOST OF OUR SONGS ARE ABOUT REAL CHARACTERS. SOMETIMES THEIR NAMES APPEAR WITHOUT US EVEN REALISING IT,' HE REPLIED.

'Matinee' captures romantic escapism via dizzying wordplay, including an ironic take on fame, by the end of which Alex is singing about 'Telling Terry Wogan how I made it'.

107

One reviewer, however, pointed out a weakness in what was otherwise an excellent, if short, debut: 'Franz Ferdinand's weakness, if they have one, may be their archness, and the fine line they walk between enjoyably daft art rock and ironically-mustachioed ridiculousness.'

Franz Ferdinand, however, were enjoying their so called ridiculousness. It was this overblown playfulness – so at odds with regular rock bands, who often took themselves far too seriously – which was central to their appeal. By January 2005 the album had sold 3.2 million copies worldwide.

The group were again switching intermittently between indulging in the ideas and inspiration that they so enjoyed, and trying to deflate their own cleverness. The video for 'Take Me Out' belonged in both camps. Inspired by the Dadaist constructivist movement and Monty Python, it was also a fun pop video that focuses on a fight between two boxers in a picture of a newspaper article entitled 'Franz vs. Anti-Franz'.

SURPRISE, SURPRISE, FRANZ IS BEATING THE SHIT OUT OF HIS OPPONENTS.

The album was definitely over the top, if not operatic in style. But this was often undercut by Alex's ironic lyrics, and always by the funky, dance-able nature of the tunes.

They marked its release by playing 'Take Me Out' for over 600 people at a record signing in the Virgin Megastore in Glasgow. Paula Brady, 21, from Glasgow, who'd had to queue up for hours in a biting wind made it clear what she thought:

'THEY ARE BRILLIANT. THEY ARE A REAL BAND WITH REAL SONGS.'

The band were genuinely touched by her endorsement.

The band had grown to such an amazing extent in the latter parts of 2003/early 2004 that they spawned their own fan site which was desperate to conduct an interview with them. They were asked by the site how they were coping with their new found fame:

Alex: **'I find it strange when people come up and ask for my autograph 'cos I'm just an ordinary guy. But we can just about do autographs now – we practiced them for years on the dole and we're pretty down to pat with them now.'**

The next question was whether the band would have bought their debut album themselves:

ALEX: 'ABSOLUTELY.'
PAUL: 'I'D BORROW IT AND TAPE IT.'
BOB: 'I'D DOWNLOAD IT. FUCK BUYING RECORDS, THAT'S FOR SAPS.'

Franz Ferdinand have only recently become involved in the debate over illegal file sharing. Bob's comment is blatantly on the side of the pirates, but Alex has also started to defend them with the rather dubious rationale that such people also buy.

He told **Rolling Stone**: 'Downloading is a great way to find out about music. I'm not going to criticise somebody for loving music. People come up to me and say, "I downloaded your album, and I can't wait to go out and buy it".'

In March 2005, Roadrunner Records, the label who in 1997 had signed and quickly dropped Alex's old band, The Karelia, decided to cash in on Franz Ferdinand's growing fame, and resurrect their only album, *Divorce at High Noon*. The album was re-released after it sparked bidding frenzies among diehard Franz fans on eBay.

Alex was furious and told the **Daily Mirror**: 'They dropped us – they completely deleted all trace of us. I'd rather people downloaded it from the Internet than bought it off those fuckers.'

Spring saw the band embark on their world tour, beginning in the Netherlands, where they played at the huge Paradiso venue in Amsterdam, but didn't neglect the smaller ones in places such as Rotterdam and Utrecht.

During another brief visit to America in March '04, the quartet signed the rights to their U.S record releases to Epic, part of the Sony corporation.

It was left to Alex to work a line to the fans that stressed their commitment to Domino and not money:

'When we signed to Domino it was for the whole world and because Domino is a small independent label, it uses other companies in different countries to put the records out. We had been going out on Domino records in the States, but the U.S branch of Domino is only three guys in an office, so we enlisted the help of Epic in America because we liked their attitude. The most important thing was that they didn't want to change anything at all about Domino or our relationship with Domino.'

Epic had world famous artists such as AC/DC, Audioslave and Jamiroquai on their books before acquiring Franz Ferdinand. The band may well have liked Epic's attitude. What they liked even more was their money. The band took a £1.5 million for signing with Epic.

When asked about it, Alex said, 'It's vulgar to talk about money.'

When pressed with the reported sum, he retorted, 'It's actually fifty quid.'

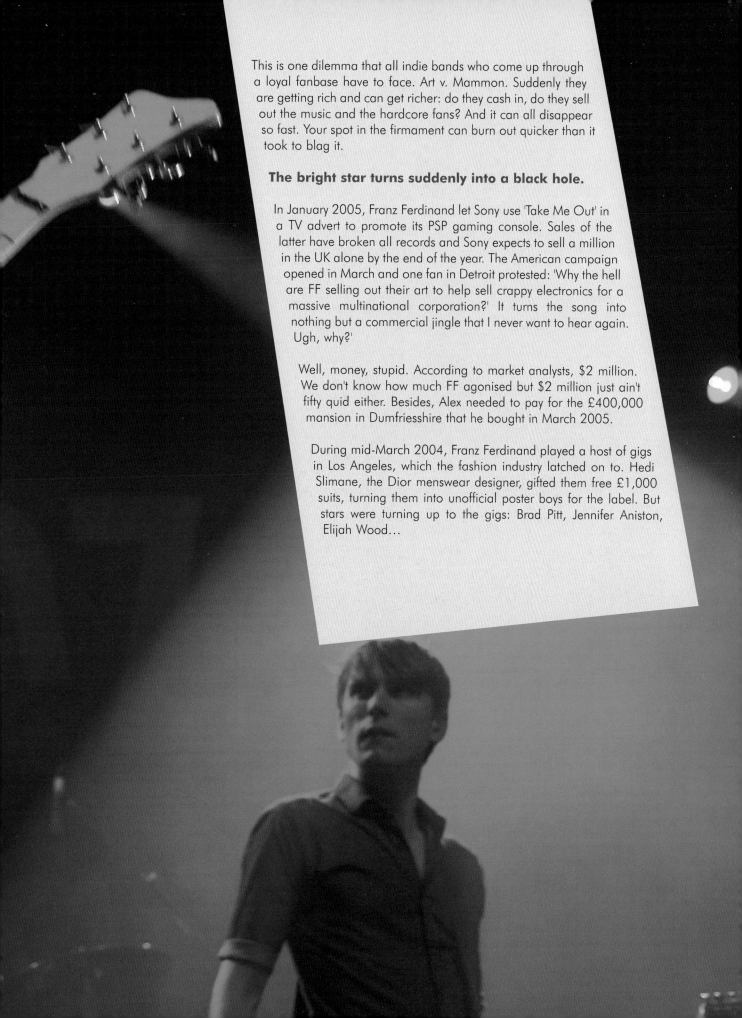

This is one dilemma that all indie bands who come up through a loyal fanbase have to face. Art v. Mammon. Suddenly they are getting rich and can get richer: do they cash in, do they sell out the music and the hardcore fans? And it can all disappear so fast. Your spot in the firmament can burn out quicker than it took to blag it.

The bright star turns suddenly into a black hole.

In January 2005, Franz Ferdinand let Sony use 'Take Me Out' in a TV advert to promote its PSP gaming console. Sales of the latter have broken all records and Sony expects to sell a million in the UK alone by the end of the year. The American campaign opened in March and one fan in Detroit protested: 'Why the hell are FF selling out their art to help sell crappy electronics for a massive multinational corporation?' It turns the song into nothing but a commercial jingle that I never want to hear again. Ugh, why?'

Well, money, stupid. According to market analysts, $2 million. We don't know how much FF agonised but $2 million just ain't fifty quid either. Besides, Alex needed to pay for the £400,000 mansion in Dumfriesshire that he bought in March 2005.

During mid-March 2004, Franz Ferdinand played a host of gigs in Los Angeles, which the fashion industry latched on to. Hedi Slimane, the Dior menswear designer, gifted them free £1,000 suits, turning them into unofficial poster boys for the label. But stars were turning up to the gigs: Brad Pitt, Jennifer Aniston, Elijah Wood…

There was also the problem with slag-hag *celeb-ettes* looking for a rising-star fame ticket. Sadie Frost, Jude Law's ex, and supermodel Kate Moss both auditioned for Alex but he reacted as if his mother had suggested something unthinkable. As for meeting Chris Martin and Gwyneth Paltrow Alex just commented, 'We'll be civil, but the idea of a celebrity love match is just ridiculous.'

Then they headed the line-up at the Astoria venue. **Xfm** urged people to '…for once believe the hype. Franz Ferdinand is what you've been waiting for. Watch them set the world alight the same way they burnt the Astoria tonight. In a word: phenomenal.' The only glitch in the performance came when an excited female threw her bra onto the stage. Alex deliberately missed a line to convey his shock at seeing such a garment in public, but he was soon laddishly throwing the undergarment at his colleagues. But from the beginning they had made it clear they were not going to become sexually entangled in the discarded underwear of female fans.

In the same month of April, Paul married his long-time girlfriend, Esther Congreave, in London. It was a quiet Registry Office ceremony but about thirty of them celebrated that evening in a restaurant in Hackney. Everyone chipped some cash for the bill as, although the four were on the edge of being very rich, they were actually only drawing a wage of £250 each per week. Paul topped up the whip-round with a £200 cheque. It bounced. It would be a few months before Esther could say, 'It's nice not to be supporting Paul anymore.'

When people asked him what is was like being married, his reply was: 'I have to say I've no idea. We had our honeymoon in Blackpool – I just couldn't face getting on another flight.'

Bands always have to deal with the groupie issue. Of course, for many rock 'n' rollers it isn't an issue, just a perk of the work. For some reason, which astonishingly *The Sun* hasn't yet given us the inside griff on, **many teenage girls find that rock stars, festivals and, perhaps, some good ol' mood-enhancing drugs fuel a nympho trip that would give their parents, if they knew, the primal screams.** Franz Ferdinand had always followed a loose rule of keeping backstage groupie-free, but at their first Glastonbury, where all the groupies romp around for their bragging rights like freebie hookers on heat, they made this explicit. No groupies.

Alex said on the subject, 'Our principal goal is to make girls dance, unlike many bands whose sole aim is to make girls sleep with them… we're all quite romantic guys and prefer real love rather than being in some squalid dressing room with someone you've never spoken to.' This provoked some of the press that traffic in this kind of thing to accuse them of being very 'un-rock 'n' roll'. Alex talks of one of the real perks: 'In the last year, things have really taken off and all of a sudden you get to meet all your heroes Bowie, Morrissey, Jarvis Cocker.'

Meanwhile Alex was cosying up to Eleanor Friedberger of the Fiery Furnaces. The latter were now supporting FF rather than the other way round. In one interview with **NME** magazine he was asked about the rumours concerning him and Eleanor to which he replied, 'It's true both sing in bands.'

The appearances on *Top of the Pops* were coming thick and fast. At one of these appearances, Alex stopped to look at arsey white rapper Eminem, which caused his 28-stone minder to shout 'Keep moving'. Alex stood his ground and kept looking at Eminem 'even though I wasn't interested in him'.

The minder decided to take him out and just jumped on Alex, **but the tub of lard seemed to melt around the beanpole singer who remained standing.** A punch-up then ensued between Eminem's security and Alex and the rest of Franz Ferdinand who piled in. **Eminem was under his dresser in a quivering heap.** TV personnel separated the combatants. Afterwards there was much comment about the white tough-guy rapper being '**all mouth and not even any trousers**'.

Alex claims not to have a quick tempter but accepts he has '…a low bullshit tolerance and like winding up idiots. Sometimes my mouth gets engaged before my brain, so while I was thinking to myself, "This guy is five times my weight," I was mouthing off at him anyway. I suppose I was the equivalent of a fly buzzing round his head. The only thing that saved me from being completely flattened was Nick.'

Franz Ferdinand
DO YOU WANT TO

The touring continued non-stop and all over the world. They did a short trip down under to play at the Melbourne Palace as well as venues in Sydney and New South Wales in yet another series of sold-out gigs. The band couldn't believe that they were getting the same fan worship and critical acclaim on the either side of the planet that they got in Britain. Their only setback was at the airport in Auckland, New Zealand, where they were caught unwittingly trying to smuggle an orange into the country.

As their baggage went through baggage control, the computerised X-ray machines, presumably programmed to fruit and veg, triggered the alarm. A security guard pounced on their bags and located the offending orange, holding it aloft in triumph like it was the head of Osama bin Laden. The four cracked up partly in relief since, as Alex said, the band '...thought they've found the stash of cocaine.' But the relief turned to disbelief when they were fined 200 Australian dollars.

In September, Franz Ferdinand were awarded the Mercury Prize, with a £20,000 cheque, for their debut album. They were 'gobsmacked [and] chuffed' as they weren't expecting to win and didn't prepare an acceptance speech. Alex picked up the award with his younger sister Anne. He noted around this time, 'In Glasgow, no one treats us any differently. There are no egos. It's as it was before.' Of course, most of it wasn't as it was before but, in respect of how those who knew them before they were famous treated them, it was. And they still paid their dues: they quietly put on unannounced concerts in the town for kids and students, and they gave the Mercury cheque to charity, too.

Alex responded to one question about fame: 'I think that the way we're all dealing with it is not considering ourselves famous, and certainly not to think of us as different people. Of course we love the fact that lots of people enjoy the music, and lots of people enjoy the shows. But you've got to keep your head about you in these situations and not let your ego inflate. You can lose all of your identity. What makes a good band good is their personality, their character, and how they portray that character through their music.

'And if they get caught up in an ego trip, they usually destroy their character.'

The band was getting hotter but the personnel were staying cool.

Well, until the gig at the Paris Zenith in November when Nick and Alex resumed hostilities from their vodka stand-off but, according to an onlooker, it was a bit 'like handbags at 50 paces'. By now they had been virtually joined at the hip for 18 months and tempers were fraying. Nick said, **'Living together 24 hours a day for a year and a half had just got to the point where if you dropped your pencil, it was the other guy's fault.'**

Nick's sartorial style had never endeared itself to Alex and one red and black striped jumper was especially offensive to his refined sensibilities. They were about to go back on stage to receive their gold discs for album sales when it erupted. Bob separated them but manager Cerne Canning had a word…

Once when Bob was asked who his all-time favourite dictator is, he replied, 'The big man himself, Cerne Canning.' Canning has been managing bands for over 20 years and he has been a crucial background factor in the Franz Ferdinand phenom. He knows every rope in the game. 'I think reality gets very blurred with a lot of bands: there's so many temptations. Often musicians are very young, even the people around them are very young… There's a lot to be said for the vitality of youth, and quite often fucking-up or experiencing things is the best way of finding out what's good; but equally it's why there are an awful lot of short-lived careers, and why there are an awful lot of casualties… and that's not really showing any signs of changing.'

He wants to pilot Franz Ferdinand to becoming a long-term entity, which he knows will be a lot harder than their current success. Cerne knows that there are all manner of elusive qualities that make or break top bands: the chemistry of how the members interact being one. And this can be upset by success itself. The pressure especially from the record companies to exploit the immediate success of a band is intense. The way they do can unbalance the dynamic of a group. 'Often record companies, and the business side of music,' he notes, **'exploit the ego thing within groups in terms of controlling people: they make singers very important, everyone else very unimportant.'**

FF are international but '...they don't want to lose the reality of what they're about, and their world, which was very important to the inception of the band, and very important to the identity of the band... I think that comes across in the music: there's a certain romanticism, but there's also a lot of reality and first-hand experience, both pleasant and unpleasant, and I think that reflects Glasgow.'

Canning's job is to keep them '**...motivated, but you want to keep people grounded, and doing these two things when success comes is very difficult.**'

And the success was coming thick and fast. In 2004, they did roughly 300 concerts in places as different as Japan, New Zealand and Mexico; their album sold over 2 million and by the time their second one was released, in October 2005, 3.3 million. The name of it is the same as the first one, Franz Ferdinand, the main difference is in the colour scheme: unlike the first album, which was dark brown, orange and cream, it is black, red and pale green.

In early February they took two of the top Brit awards: Best Rock Band and Best Rock Act. They got three nominations in the 2005 Grammy Awards: Best Rock Performance, Best Short Form Video for 'Take Me Out' and Best Alternative Album but, in mid-February, took none. However, in the same month, at the NME awards they took two: Best Album and Best Track Titles.

In February Alex was invited to speak at the Edinburgh Lectures. He sat down with a bunch of classical musicians and academics at a forum on Scotland's role in 21st century music. While talking about breaking down the barriers between pop and classical, he revealed his own tastes: 'Because I listen to Nirvana and Korn I am a troubled individual, but **I'm riddled with angst because I listen to Chopin and Debussy**... I listen to Kylie Minogue and Scissor Sisters because I am upbeat and I like to party, and **I listen to Wagner because I like the smell of napalm in the morning.**'

Meanwhile, while the new album was beginning to take shape, they were touring. In May, they did two gigs in Moscow and one in St Petersburg, their sets included four numbers for the forthcoming album, these were recorded and put on a website for download. On returning from Moscow Alex, who was travelling on his Huntley passport, was detained at the airport for being 'a high level security risk'. The renegade ex-MI6 agent, Richard Tomlinson, often used the alias 'Alex Huntley'. Alex was detained for an hour before it was sorted.

The band played Glastonbury at the end of June, this time wearing their awareness wristbands: anti-bullying, Teenage Cancer Trust and make poverty history. Of course, for some time, Chris Martin had been using the Coldplay set and the back of his hand to 'Make Trade Fair'. But the competition was hotting up for who was going to be invited to play Geldof's Live 8 concert scheduled for the following month, July. Liam Gallagher had made his position clear about 'knobhead students' trying change the world but, as was pointed out, his opinion on bracelets was compromised by the fact that the only ones he'd ever worn had been put on by the police.

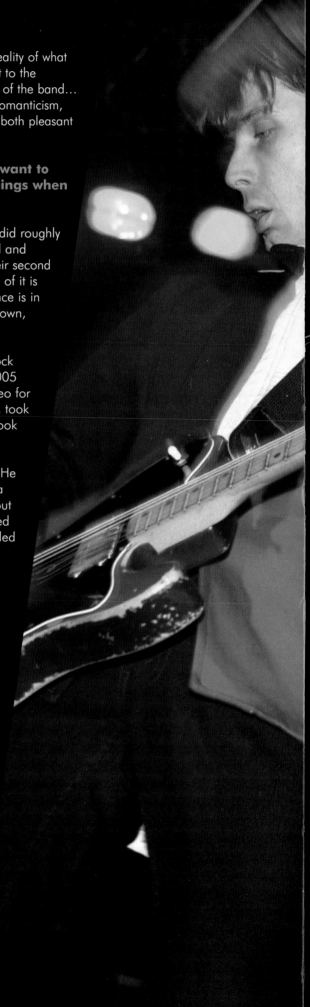

In the event, although Geldof tried hard, Franz Ferdinand had to decline because Nick and Manuela were due to marry in Germany on July 2nd. 'After all,' Nick said, 'your wedding is the biggest day of your life. Although Live 8 is a wonderful thing and an incredibly important event, personally speaking, it's not as important as your wedding.'

Gradually, there were more and more leaks and hype about the new album, which was scheduled for release on October 3rd. Much of it had been recorded at Alex's new home, a mock-Tudor farmhouse in Moniaive, Dumfriesshire, where between gigs the four regularly convened before going to New York to mix the final tracks in studio. Alex also swatted off attempts to categorise the band as 'art rock': 'People always call us arty. What the hell does that mean? Its not like we got a band together as some kind of conceptual abstract sound sculpture. We got together to make a pop band.'

There is a lot of Dylan, Bowie and Roxy Music in the sound of the new album but it is still predominantly Franz Ferdinand. The songs are rooted in their Glasgow background, even though only Paul is a native Scot. 'You Could Have It So Much Better' is about the people of Glasgow… 'I'm Your Villain' is about some a mate of Alex's who told him about a female friend's sexual encounter, 'She was lying naked on her back, and this guy tipped a bag of crisps on her belly and then poured a can of lager over them, and started licking the soggy mess.'

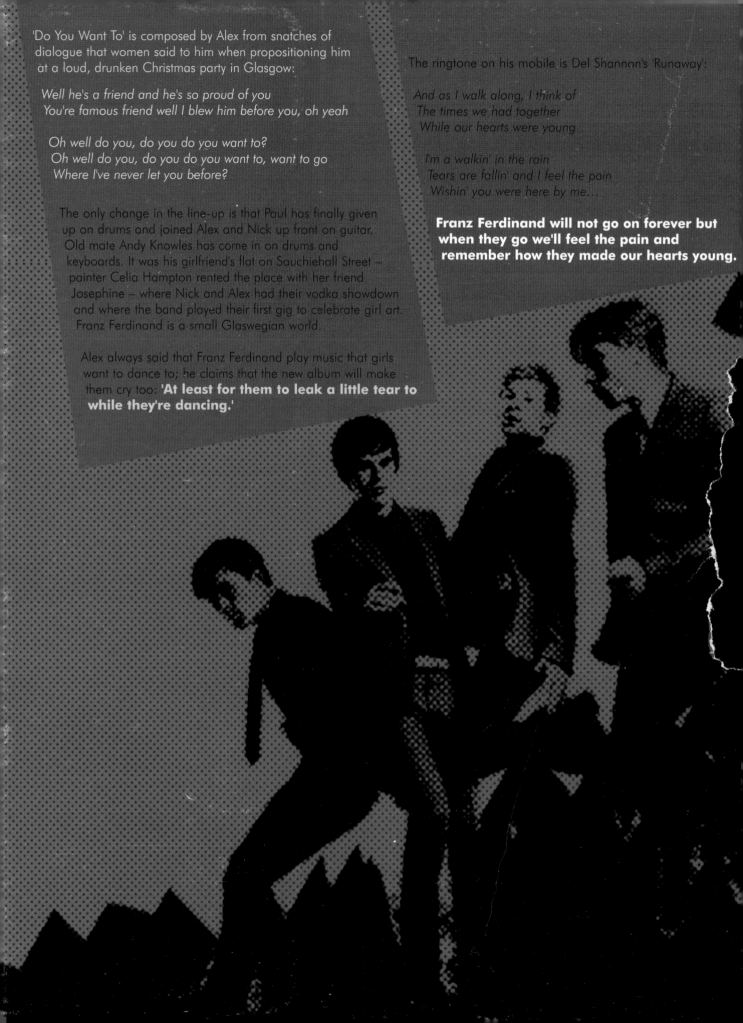

'Do You Want To' is composed by Alex from snatches of dialogue that women said to him when propositioning him at a loud, drunken Christmas party in Glasgow:

Well he's a friend and he's so proud of you
You're famous friend well I blew him before you, oh yeah

Oh well do you, do you do you want to?
Oh well do you, do you do you want to, want to go
Where I've never let you before?

The only change in the line-up is that Paul has finally given up on drums and joined Alex and Nick up front on guitar. Old mate Andy Knowles has come in on drums and keyboards. It was his girlfriend's flat on Sauchiehall Street — painter Celia Hampton rented the place with her friend Josephine — where Nick and Alex had their vodka showdown and where the band played their first gig to celebrate girl art. Franz Ferdinand is a small Glaswegian world.

Alex always said that Franz Ferdinand play music that girls want to dance to; he claims that the new album will make them cry too: **'At least for them to leak a little tear to while they're dancing.'**

The ringtone on his mobile is Del Shannon's 'Runaway':

And as I walk along, I think of
The times we had together
While our hearts were young

I'm a walkin' in the rain
Tears are fallin' and I feel the pain
Wishin' you were here by me...

Franz Ferdinand will not go on forever but when they go we'll feel the pain and remember how they made our hearts young.